POE IN 90 MINUTES

Poe
IN 90 MINUTES

Paul Strathern

IVAN R. DEE
CHICAGO

 For information, address: Ivan R. Dee, Publisher, 1332 North Halsted Street, Chicago 60622. Manufactured in the United States of America and printed on acid-free paper.

www.ivanrdee.com

Library of Congress Cataloging-in-Publication Data:
Strathern, Paul, 1940–
Poe in 90 minutes / Paul Strathern.
p. cm. — (Great writers in 90 minutes)
Includes index.
ISBN-13: 978-1-56663-691-9 (cloth : alk. paper)
ISBN-10: 1-56663-691-4 (cloth : alk. paper)
ISBN-13: 978-1-56663-690-2 (pbk. : alk. paper)
ISBN-10: 1-56663-690-6 (pbk. : alk. paper)
1. Poe, Edgar Allan, 1809–1849. I. Title. II. Title: Poe in ninety minutes.
PS2631.S85 2006
818'.309—dc22

2006019763

Contents

POE IN 90 MINUTES

Introduction

On June 30, 1849, the forty-year-old Edgar Allan Poe set out by steamboat from New York to Philadelphia, en route for Richmond, Virginia, where he hoped to raise funds and generate publicity for a new literary magazine he intended to launch. For several years he had been showing signs of mental deterioration. The death of his young wife Virginia two years earlier had been followed by a period of emotional instability, during which he had become involved in a number of entanglements with middle-aged women, some widowed, others still married. All received rapturous love poems or letters, and there is no doubting the strength of feeling these expressed—despite the fact that he was sometimes sending equally ardent missives to two of them simultaneously.

At the same time Poe was also deeply involved in writing his self-proclaimed masterpiece *Eureka: An Essay on the Material and Spiritual Universe*, in which he attempted his "explanation" of the world and its workings in one hundred heavily argued pages. Fully convinced that he had succeeded in this attempt, he wrote to his former mother-in-law, Maria Clemm: "I have no desire to live since I have done 'Eureka.' I could accomplish nothing more." He was convinced that he had discovered the secret of the universe, no less.

When Poe arrived in Philadelphia on July 1 he was suffering from delusions, raving about a group of men who had tried to kill him on the journey, declaiming passages from *Eureka*, and insisting that he had been locked up in Moyamensing Prison where he had seen visions. As he explained later, in a letter to Mrs. Clemm:

> For more than ten days I was totally deranged, although I was drinking not one drop; and during this interval I imaged the most horrible calamities. All was hallucination, arising from an attack which I had never before experienced—an attack of *mania-à-potu*.

On July 14 Poe finally arrived in Richmond, where he set about trying to raise funds for his projected magazine. During the course of his activities he encountered his former childhood sweetheart, Sarah Elmira Royster, who was now widowed. After a whirlwind romance, she promised to marry him. To Poe, it seemed that his great troubles were over; his fiancée was rich, would support him, and was willing to help finance his magazine. Apart from a couple of lapses, during which he once again reverted to becoming "horribly drunk and discoursing *Eureka* to the audiences of the Bar Rooms," he seemed to have his alchoholism under control.

On September 9 Poe gathered with friends on the veranda of the Hygeia Hotel. An eyewitness described the scene:

> The old Hygeia stood some distance from the water, but with nothing between it and the ocean. It was moonlight and the light shone over everything with that undimmed light that it has in the South. . . . Our little party was absolutely cut off from everything except that lovely view of the water shining in the moonlight and its gentle music borne to us on the soft breeze.

Poe gave a recital of his poems, which included excerpts from "Ulalume" and his most celebrated verse, "The Raven":

> "Prophet!" said I, "thing of evil!—prophet still, if bird or devil!—
> Whether Tempter sent, or whether tempest tossed thee here ashore,
> Desolate, yet all undaunted, on this desert land enchanted—
> On this home by Horror haunted,—tell me truly, I implore—

> Is there—*is* there balm in Gilead?—tell me—tell me, I implore!"
> Quoth the Raven, "Nevermore."

Poe's recital was rapturously received by his small, largely female audience of friends.

Just over two weeks later, on September 27, he set off by ship for New York, aiming to put his affairs in order before his wedding. What happened during the next three days remains for the most part a mystery. On October 3, polling day in the congressional elections at Baltimore, Poe's friend Dr. Snodgrass received a message:

> There is a gentleman, rather the worse for wear, at Ryan's 4th ward polls, who goes under the cognomen of Edgar A. Poe, and who appears in great distress, and says he is acquainted with you, and I assure you he is in need of immediate assistance.

Poe was found drunk and unconscious, wearing a thin ragged suit that was not his own, his body apparently unwashed for several days. Someone suggested that he had been drugged, or slipped alchohol, by election agents, who had led him from booth to booth to register "repeater" votes, and had then abandoned him in the gutter. Poe was rushed to the Washington College Hospital in Baltimore, where he eventually regained consciousness and began addressing "spectral and imaginary objects on the walls" before succumbing to delerium and finally lapsing into unsciousness once more. Four days later, at around five in the morning, he cried out, "God help my poor soul!" and then expired.

Some time previously Poe had entrusted his literary works to his friend Dr. Rufus W. Griswold, little suspecting that Griswold was in fact highly jealous of Poe's abilities and harbored an intense and secret hatred of him. With Poe dead, Griswold set about doing his best to ruin his reputation, writing letters to the newspapers (under pseudonyms) that blackened Poe's name and doing his utmost to sabotage Poe's literary heritage. Four years later the great French poet Charles Baudelaire would see in Poe a kindred soul, and would embark upon a campaign that would eventually bring Poe recognition in Paris, then the literary capital of the world, as one of the leading figures of his age and the finest writer America had yet produced.

Poe's biography reads at times like a parody of the life of a Romantic poet. High tragedy is intermingled with high farce; only the suffering seems to remain a constant feature, ever escalating—acting as both an inspiration and a warning against the perils of intoxication and the heroism of the literary life lived in extremis. Poe's life was short and self-destructive, yet it produced work that remains as involving and effective today as it was when he first wrote it, work that in its own way changed the face of literature. His tale "The Murders in the Rue Morgue" invented the modern detective story, a genre he developed almost to the full extent of its form. Sherlock Holmes and the classic whodunits of Agatha Christie, as well as the crimes investigated by Georges Simenon's psychologically adept sleuth Inspector Maigret, all owe a supreme debt to Poe. Likewise his development of the mystery story and the thriller, which would become staples of popular literature. Many also see his tale "The Unparalleled Adventure of One Hans

Pfaall" as the first genuine work of science fiction. Yet what Poe produced was always something more than just popular literature. Like so many of its practitioners, Poe unashamedly wrote for money: a constant and nagging preoccupation throughout his mostly impoverished existence. But at the same time he also managed to retain an almost naive belief in the highest aspirations of literature. He never abandoned his belief that literature was a lofty calling, intended to embody humanity's spirit and heroism as well as its greatest flaws and fears—a calling that required everything of those who chose to follow it, a calling where even life itself might have to be sacrificed to art. Although Poe died almost half a century before Van Gogh, his life—and the intensity of his work—can be seen very much as the literary equivalent of the troubled Dutch artist. Both would die prematurely, self-destructively—Poe at forty, Van Gogh at thirty-seven—their minds disintegrating yet at the height of their considerable powers.

Poe's Life and Works

Edgar Allan Poe was born on January 9, 1809, in Boston, Massachusetts, the son of two repertory actors who worked for a traveling stage company which performed popular dramas in theatres up and down the East Coast. His twenty-five-year-old father, David Poe, was of Irish stock, a flamboyant, impetuous character, given to drink, who played romantic supporting roles. While Edgar was still an infant, his father abandoned his mother, leaving her with three children, and simply vanished into the vastness of newly independent America, never to be heard of again.

Poe's mother Elizabeth was English; she had been widowed before her marriage to David Poe and was also a talented actress whose ethereal beauty ensured her a succession of leading roles. The infant Poe appears to have been deeply fixated on his mother, but she fell ill and died when he was just two. From then on, throughout his life, Poe would be drawn toward a succession of ethereal women, with whom he would fall platonically in love. But now the orphaned Edgar was taken into the family of John Allen, a prosperous Richmond merchant. In 1815, when Edgar was six, John Allen took his family across the Atlantic on business, traveling through Scotland and England, where Edgar studied at a number of schools, ending up at an academy for young gentlemen in suburban Stoke Newington, just outside east London. Here he did well in history and literature, though his grade report described him as "intelligent, wayward and wilful."

In 1820 the tobacco trade suffered a recession which adversely affected John Allen's business, and the family returned to live in

Richmond. During the long hot summer Poe learned to swim in Shokoe Creek and read *Robinson Crusoe*, which enthralled him. When John Allen's business improved, the family moved into a mansion with servants, and Poe was sent to a private school for the education of young Southern gentlemen, where he did well at running and boxing; around this time he is said to have swum six miles up the James River against the tide. He also fell in love with the fifteen-year-old Sarah Elmira Royster, then left to attend the University of Virginia. Here John Allen gave him only a small allowance, which severely undercut his expectations and self-image as a Southern gentleman. Mixing with the sons of wealthy plantation owners, he soon ran up gambling debts, then gambled further in the attempt to recoup them, running up even more serious debts. At the same time he began drinking, a pastime to which he was physiologically unsuited as he tended to get drunk after a single glass of wine.

In December 1826 Poe returned to Richmond to find that his beloved Sarah had become engaged to someone else. John Allen was furious when he learned of Poe's drinking and gambling debts, and refused to allow him to return to the university. This marked the beginning of Poe's serious difficulties with his guardian. Temperamentally the hardheaded businessman, Allen was the polar opposite of Poe, who had now begun to write romantic poetry of a distinctly Byronic turn:

> I stand amid the roar
> Of a surf-tormented shore,
> And I hold within my hand
> Grains of the golden sand—
> How few! Yet how they creep
> Through my fingers to the deep. . . .

Poe now left home, sailing north for Boston, where he met a printer who agreed to publish a book of his poems in an edition of about four dozen copies: *Tamerlane and Other Poems* by "A Bostonian" appeared in May 1827. Poe was only eighteen, and this was very much an apprentice work; despite his natural pride and unmistakable ambition, he was well aware of this fact, leading him to include a somewhat awkward and ambiguous disclaimer in the Preface: "The greater part of the Poems which compose this little volume were written in 1821–2, when the author had not completed his fourteenth year. They were of course not intended for publication; why they are now published concerns no one but himself: they perhaps savour too much of Egotism; but they were written by one too young to have any knowledge of the world but for his own heart." Needless to say, most if not all of these poems were in fact written well after "his fourteenth year" (when he would have been just thirteen years old). The majority of them were heavily influenced by the English Romantic poets, some to the extent where Poe's "borrowings" verge on plagiarism; such influences may not yet have been absorbed, but there is no doubting the poet's heartfelt empathy for the likes of Coleridge and Shelley, and his understanding that this was the direction in which he wished to develop his poetic persona. The opening lines of the short poem "Imitation" are typical in their quality and tenor:

> A dark unfathomed tide
> Of interminable pride—
> A mystery, and a dream
> Should my early life seem. . . .

Perhaps only with hindsight can one see promise in such lines; but what for many a teenager would be a gauche phase would in Poe's case deepen into something more profound. The title poem "Tamerlane" was named after the fabled Mongol warrior who conquered Russia and India in the fourteenth century, a typical Romantic self-identification.

By November 1827 Poe had run out of money, and in an effort to retain his independence he took the drastic step of enlisting in the army, under the name of Edgar A. Perry. He served in South Carolina and later in Virginia, where in January 1829 he was promoted to sergeant-major; but three months later he left the service. By now his foster mother had died in Richmond; John Allen would soon remarry, causing Poe to feel like a stranger when he returned to the Allen household. That summer Poe went to Baltimore and lived with his maternal aunt, Maria Clemm, and her six-year-old daughter Virginia.

In December 1829 Poe published *Al Aaraaf, Tamerlane, and Minor Poems*, this time under the name Edgar A. Poe. The seventy-one-page volume contained revisions of "Tamerlane" and some of his earlier poems, as well as many striking new poems in what was now becoming recognizable as an increasingly personal style. The title poem, "Al Aaraaf," displayed a growing technical facility with differences of meter and ambitious romantic coloring, though these frequently obscured the meaning. As a result, the poem has been interpreted in many different ways. Most critics concur, however, that this was an attempt to articulate, in allegorical fashion, Poe's aesthetic theories as well as his view that the poetic imagination appeared doomed in the increasingly materialistic world he saw growing up around him.

> He was a goodly spirit—he who fell:
> A wanderer by mossy mantled well—
> A gazer on the lights that shine above—
> A dreamer in the moonbeam by his love:
> What wonder? for each star is eye-like there,
> And looks so sweetly down on Beauty's hair—

Few sergeant-majors, before or since, can have entertained such sentiments or penned such lines.

By contrast, Poe also included a number of humorous poems which were intended to parody his dark romantic view of the world.

> Dim vales—and shadowy floods—
> And cloudy-looking woods,
> Whose forms we can't discover
> For all the tears that drip all over.
> Huge moons there wax and wane—
> Again—again—again— . . .

These humorous poems show a deepening maturity replacing his earlier hesitancy, indicating that he now had a more profound self-awareness, though this still included a remnant of callow self-doubt. Despite this, there is nothing tongue-in-cheek about the poem "To Helen," which would become one of his best-remembered poems in its later version, which opens:

> Helen, thy beauty is to me
> Like those Nicean barks of yore,
> That gently, o'er a perfumed sea,
> The weary, way-worn wanderer bore
> To his own native shore.

Such lines are characteristic in their evocative power, which intentionally reverts to ancient usage such as "of yore" (together with the unfortunate hostage to fortune "bore"). As so often in Poe's poetry, sublime aspiration is frequently marred by uninspired realization; but it was just such aspiration that was shaping the literary persona which would take flight in the less exalted medium of prose.

With the intention of setting Poe on course for a respectable military career, John Allen helped get his stepson into West Point, but the atmosphere and discipline of this crack military academy proved uncongenial to Poe. He took refuge in spinning yarns about his experiences in South America. His fellow students soon saw through these purely imaginary tales and began regarding him as an oddball. Their view was confirmed when Poe decided he had had enough of West Point and proceeded to get himself expelled, cutting drill parades and classes whenever possible. According to one anecdote, when he was specifically ordered to report for parade wearing "white belt and gloves, under arms," Poe decided to obey this order to the letter. He appeared wearing belt and gloves, with his rifle slung over his arm, but otherwise naked. As a consequence of this and other incidents, he was expelled from West Point in February 1831 for "gross neglect of duty."

That summer Poe returned to Baltimore and lived with Maria Clemm and her daughter. He now began writing short stories and tales, initially with the aim of simply earning money to support himself, and in the following year the *Philadelphia Saturday Courier* published five of his tales. But this hardly earned enough to support him and Mrs. Clemm, who was herself impoverished. In April 1833 he wrote a despairing letter to his guardian, which is worth quoting at length for the light it sheds on Poe's difficult relationship with Allen:

> It has now been more than two years since you have assisted me, and more than three since you have spoken to me. . . . If you will only consider in what situation I am placed you will surely pity me—without friends, without any means consequently of obtaining employment, I am perishing. . . . And yet I am not idle—nor addicted to any vice—nor have I committed any offence against society. . . . For God's sake pity me, and save me from destruction.
>
> E. A. Poe

Apparently Allen did not reply to this plea from the abyss. He soon became ill with dropsy, and was confined to an armchair in his bedroom, forbidden all visitors and attended by nurses. In desperation, Poe decided to follow up his letter with a visit to Richmond where he rang the bell to Allen's house. The door was answered by Allen's wife, who was shocked by Poe's "remarkable appearance"; she told him that her husband was not in a fit state to see him. But Poe brushed past her and ran up the stairs to Allen's bedroom, followed by Mrs. Allen. According to her, "As soon as [Poe] entered the chamber, Mr. Allen raised his cane, and threatening to strike him if he came within reach, ordered him out; upon which Poe withdrew; and that was the last time they ever met." Not long after this, John Allen died; despite his considerable wealth, there was no mention of Poe in his will.

But by now Poe had achieved his first small taste of literary success. In October 1833 his tale "MS. Found in a Bottle" won a competition in the *Baltimore Sunday Visiter*. The prize money may have been just fifty dollars (not such a mean sum in those days), but more important it brought his work to a wider audience and his name to the notice of influential editors. Poe had in fact entered six stories for this competition, and the judges were almost equally impressed by those that did not win the prize, expressing the hope that they would all soon be published together as a book—though circumstances would conspire against this happening for another seven years.

"MS. Found in a Bottle" is a compelling and accomplished blend of reality and the supernatural. It has thrills and suspense, and leads the reader into the realms of sheer terror; despite such excitement, at all times it retains its factual conviction. The story is cast as a message, which purports to be from an anonymous but learned traveler: "Of my country and of my family I have little to say." The text hints that he may well have been of Germanic origin, with a taste for skeptical philosophy: "I have often been reproached for the aridity of my genius; a deficiency of imagination has been imputed to me as a crime." This unimaginative writer begins with a blend of the exotic and the banal; the author of the note in the bottle is used to visiting distant parts of the globe, which he now views with little wonder. "After many years spent in foreign travel, I sailed in the year 18—, from the port of

Batavia, in the rich and populous island of Java, on a voyage to the Archipelago of the Sunda islands. . . . Our vessel was a beautiful ship of about four hundred tons, copper-fastened and built at Bombay of Malabar teak." The reader is immediately grabbed, wondering what will disturb this outward calm—what caused the traveler to entrust this note to a bottle, what happened next? This is Romantic literature from an age when a writer could aspire to be both a storyteller and an artist. Even Poe's admired English poets were not afraid to spin their art into a good story: Coleridge wrote of journeying to Xanadu, Shelley of the fallen statue of Ozymandias in the desert, Byron of adventures in Italy. Literature was popular in both senses of the word: it attracted a large audience and was not shy about entertaining its readers. Such a stage was made for Poe's talents. Here all the inner fears and uncertainties of his unstable character could be given free rein, and in the process the weak, suffering, and often despairing man could transform himself into the heroic integrated persona of an artist.

Another tale that Poe wrote at this time was "The Unparalleled Adventure of One Hans Pfaal," which describes a journey to the Moon in a balloon. It was originally intended as a parody of the fanciful, highly unscientific tales of travel to other planets that were popular at the time. As Poe began telling the story, however, he could not help including realistic details, in an attempt to render it scientifically plausible. From burlesque romance it became transformed into a more and more convincing description, now bordering on a hoax. Diary entries were included to lend an air of veracity:

> *April 11th.* Found a startling diminution in the apparent diameter of the earth, and a considerable increase, now observable for the first time, in that of the moon itself. . . .
>
> *April 15th.* Not even the outlines of continents and seas could now be traced upon the earth with distinctness. . . .
>
> *April 16th.* Today, looking upwards as well as I could, through each of the side windows

> alternately, I beheld, to my great delight, a very small portion of the moon's disc protruding, as it were, on all sides beyond the huge circumference of the balloon.

The resulting tale has elements of hoax, fantasy, scientific plausibility, and realistic account, as well as a self-defeating afterword which was intended to reveal all. Despite this evident muddle of motive and execution, Poe's "Hans Pfaal" has all the ingredients of an adventure story and is now regarded by some critics as the first piece of genuine science fiction.

In August 1835 Poe was able to leave Baltimore for Richmond, where he had been appointed an editor of the *Southern Literary Messenger* by its owner Thomas W. White. He soon fell out with White when he turned up for work drunk, but after an abject apology White took pity on Poe and reinstated him, on condition that he live with a respectable family "where liquor is not used." Poe sent for Maria Clemm and her daughter Virginia to join him. Virginia Clemm was now thirteen years old, but this did not prevent Poe from falling in love with her and proposing that they marry. Mrs. Clemm was of two minds about it but was eventually swayed by the evident happiness of her daughter and her beloved nephew, and gave her blessing. With the connivance of a friend, Poe obtained a certificate declaring Virginia to be "of the full age of twenty-one years," and they were married. The proud Mrs. Clemm presided over a strictly alcohol-free reception, and the newly married couple set off for a brief honeymoon in the Virginia hills.

On his return Poe was soon working all hours at the *Southern Literary Messenger*, producing a continuous stream of articles, reviews, and stories to fill its pages, as well as writing letters seeking subscriptions to the magazine. By the beginning of 1837 he had increased the readership of the magazine from 500 to 3,500, in the process making it and its editor known throughout America. Then he succumbed to the bottle once more, and White fired him; whereupon Poe set off for New York, taking his wife and mother-in-law with him. He was now sufficiently well known not to worry about his future, but once again he was to be dogged by misfortune. In the early months of 1837 America suffered a serious financial panic, bankrupting businesses and throwing many out of work. The magazines that accepted Poe's stories were soon closing down, and he was advised that his best way to make money was to write a novel. The result was the novella *The Narrative of Arthur Gordon Pym of Nantucket*, published in New York in 1838. It was the only novel that Poe would publish, and its hero was heavily based on its author—Edgar becoming Arthur, his despised middle name Allan being replaced by the family name of Lord Byron, and Poe becoming Pym. Once again, Poe turned to adventure at sea; as in "MS. Found in a Bottle," the narrative is in the first person, but it also includes entries in the narrator's journal, snippets of purely factual information, and informative footnotes. All these are intended to bolster the veracity of the story, which abounds in compelling detail, even though the narrative is often disjointed and the psychological development is rather thin. Such a curious blend has the effect of luring the reader into a world that lies somehow beyond the real, a phantasmagorical, almost hallucinatory realm of heightened sensibility and intense emotion where almost anything can happen. The result is a pervading atmosphere of fear, frequently rising to sheer terror; and the very vagueness of the story's telling has the effect of leaving it open to wide interpretation. Some have seen this novel as simply an episodic tale involving a variety of elements, including an impulsive sailing trip, prolonged incarceration in a pitch-dark hold below decks, and an Antarctic expedition, subjects whose popularity had already been established by such works as Defoe's *Robinson Crusoe* and Coleridge's *The Rhyme of the Ancient Mariner*. Others have sought allegorical or psychological interpretations, of more or less plausibility. Whether or not one believes such literary sleuthing and psychological sleight of hand, there is no denying that this work, like almost all of Poe's writing, involves deep, often unconscious elements of his personality, whose force frequently disturbs and distorts the conscious surface of the narrative. The outer world bends and buckles under the force of Poe's vision, and this very lack of distancing gives the narrative its claustrophobic, angst-ridden quality. When we are drawn into Poe's world, we are aware of entering an involving region of terrors from which there is no escape into the calm of a more objective reality. This said, *The Narrative of Arthur Gordon Pym* is not fully successful; such phantasmagorical qualities are best evoked in briefer, more tense narratives. Poe evidently realized this, for from now on he would concentrate his creative energies on shorter works.

In 1840 he finally published his collection of stories, *Tales of the Grotesque and Arabesque*, whose plainly stated aim, as outlined in the Preface, was to create "terror of the soul." This work contains several of Poe's finest stories that would ensure his literary immortality, including such memorable masterpieces as "The Fall of the House of Usher," and "Ligeia." The latter is a tale of death, human obsession, and "the will therein lieth, which dieth not." It opens in a typically factual but vague manner, which already presages a haunting presence: "I cannot, for my soul, remember how, when, or even precisely where, I first became acquainted with the lady Ligeia."

The subject of the story is taken from Poe's earlier poem "Al Aaraaf," in which Ligeia is the soul of beauty; but here the reverse side of her nature is emphasized. The intensity of the prose is heightened by the inclusion of Ligeia's poetry, which evokes such horrors as:

> But see, amid the mimic rout
>   A crawling shape intrude!
> A blood-red thing that writhes from out
>   The scenic solitude!
> It writhes!—it writhes!—with mortal pangs
>   The mimes become its food,
> And the seraphs sob at vermin fangs
>   In human gore imbued.

In a superb climax we witness the superhuman power of the dead Ligeia's will as she reaches from beyond the grave to take over the dead body of Rowena, the woman who has supplanted her as the narrator's wife. The scene is described as if from inside the head of the crazed husband, expressing his thoughts and emotions as "the fair-haired blue-eyed" Rowena becomes transformed before his eyes:

> *Had she then grown taller since her malady?* What inexpressible madness seized me with that thought? One bound, and I had reached her feet! Shrinking from my touch, she let fall from her head, unloosed . . . and there streamed forth, into the rushing atmosphere of the chamber, huge masses of long and disheveled hair. *It was blacker than the raven wings of midnight!* And now slowly opened the eyes of the figure which stood before me. . . . I shrieked aloud, "can I never—can I never be mistaken—these are the full, and the black, and the wild eyes—of my lost love—of the Lady—of the Lady Ligeia."

Poe would claim this was his finest tale, an estimation with which few critics would agree. But it is not difficult to see why he felt so strongly about "Ligeia": this was a highly psychological piece of writing, which often reads as if it is guided more by unconscious forces than the writer's deliberate intentions. In writing this tale Poe appears to have felt more in contact with his entire being, coming closer to some trauma that he sought to exorcise. His feelings for his dead mother, as well as those toward his child bride, would appear to have played a significant role in the composition of this piece of literary Grand Guignol. As Poe himself so eloquently put it: "There is no point, among the many incomprehensible anomalies of the science of mind, more thrillingly exciting than the fact—never, I believe, noticed in the schools—that in our endeavors to recall to memory something long forgotten, we often find ourselves *upon the very verge* of remembrance, without being able, in the end, to remember." Poe may have been in the grip of strong unconscious forces, but he remained ever the consummate artist, capable of perceptions and philosophical insights of the highest order.

The longer story, "The Fall of the House of Usher," is similarly powerful and in many ways more subtly atmospheric. The famous long opening sentence not only sets the scene but skilfully draws in the reader and stimulates his expectation:

> During the whole of a dull, dark, and soundless day in the autumn of the year, when the clouds hung oppressively low in the heavens, I had been passing alone, on horseback, through a singularly dreary tract of country, and at length found myself, as the shades of the evening drew on, within view of the melancholy House of Usher.

The central figure of this tale is Roderick Usher, the degenerate end of a long and noble line, whose traits and weaknesses are perceptively described. As so often, Poe is describing an aspect of himself, and even goes so far as to ascribe the authorship of one of his recently written poems to Usher. "The Haunted House" is itself classic Poe, its short narrative neatly dovetailing with the plot of the overall story, as it describes the ancient house assailed by "evil things, in robes of sorrow," which now evokes "but a dim remembered story of the old time entombed":

> And travelers now within that valley,
>   Through the red-litten windows see
> Vast forms, that move fantastically
>   To a discordant melody,
> While, like a ghastly rapid river,
>   Through the pale door,
> A hideous throng rush out forever
>   And laugh—but smile no more.

Ironically the poem is quoted as evidence of Usher's descent into madness during his long residence in this "collocation of . . . stones [and] the many *fungi* which overspread them . . . and its reduplication in the still waters of the tarn." Poe's images and metaphors constantly reflect the mind of Usher and his state, accumulating to form a penetrating and skillful piece of sustained self-analysis. Long before Freud, Poe uses the material of psychoanalysis to build an in-depth portrait of his Usher-persona. In the course of this he also lists "the books which, for years, had formed no small portion of the mental existence of the invalid." These include many of Poe's own favorite authors and works—such as Machiavelli, Swedenborg's description of his visionary travels in heaven and hell, and the "Chiromancy" of Robert Flud—as well as a number of invented authors and suggestive titles of purely imaginary works cleverly interspersed among the obscure real ones:

> One favorite volume was a small octavo edition of the "Directorium Inquisitorium" by the Dominican Eymeric de Gironne; and there were passages in Pomponius Mela, about the old African Satyrs and Ægipans, over which Usher would sit dreaming for hours. His chief delight, however, was found in the perusal of an exceedingly rare and curious book in quarto Gothic—the manual of a forgotten church—the *Vigilæ Mortuorum secundum Chorum Ecclesiæ Maguntinæ.*

The narrator finds himself drawn into the world of Roderick Usher, even going so far as to assist him in "the temporary entombment" of the body of Roderick's dead twin sister Madeline in the vaults.

It is easy to detect in this tale Poe's fears regarding his own mental disintegration. Usher's madness is certainly pieced together out of intimations and mental turbulence that Poe himself had experienced. Yet this is much more than skillfully disguised autobiography. The ingredients of the tale—the intrigued narrator, Usher himself, his twin sister Madeline, and the pervading melancholy of this grim world set amidst such forbidding wilderness—are assembled with the narrative skill of a great storyteller. The reader is drawn ever further into Usher's world by the use of underplayed suggestion and mounting suspense, yet it is precisely these thriller-writer's skills that serve to disguise the high art to which Poe constantly aspired. Psychology, philosophy, speculation, and insight are all included, but at no time do they disturb the unraveling of the tale—which remains at all times fantastic, in the sense of being a superb read as well as being imbued with something quite beyond the realm of the ordinary.

As Poe's work continued to progress from strength to strength, his life was ever more plagued by instability and humiliation. Although he managed for the most part to curb his drinking, when he did succumb his raving behavior frequently resulted in very public disgrace. It was now all too clear that alcohol was poison for Poe, and even a small quantity quickly led to a complete disintegration of his character. Such was the extreme nature of his behavior that many believed he had become a drug addict, a canard that would persist long after his death. Modern medical assessment of his behavior now suggests that his exaggerated loss of control was probably due to a brain lesion rather than opium, morphine, or any of the more colorful suggestions that so dogged his reputation. Yet it must be emphasized that it was in spite of these weaknesses that Poe now began producing such fine work. Astonishing mental resilience, the ability to rouse himself from incapacitating depression, profound self-knowledge, and concentrated willpower—all these were required, and marshaled, by the writer who enjoyed above all else the exercise of his rare creative qualities. These, and these alone, could lead him into a world where he was immune from his damning flaws, and enable him to exorcise the demons that so haunted him: what we read are the chaos of fear and neurosis—the messy phantasms of Poe's mind—given life and form by the great transforming process of art.

In the early 1840s Poe continued to edit and contribute to various magazines in cities along the East Coast. The work he produced in this period is nothing short of remarkable. With "The Murders in the Rue Morgue" Poe created the modern detective story, at the same time playing a major role in the development of this new genre. The mysterious crime that is ingeniously solved by a gentleman sleuth using only close attention to clues and his own exceptionally well-developed powers of reason is the recognizable blueprint of a literary form that would later produce such masters of rationality and attention to detail as Sherlock Holmes and Hercule Poirot, as well as innumerable lesser figures.

Poe's original sleuth was Monsieur C. Auguste Dupin—another loose transformation of his own name: C for "vision," Auguste a French upgrading of Allan, and Du-pin a recognizable echo of Poe. Such identification aided Poe, enabling him to expand and examine his central character while retaining the unity of a coherent persona. Dupin lives in Paris and is a creature of pure intellect and awareness, proceeding step by logical step, his mind unsullied by unnecessary emotion or illogical conjecture. This was how Poe liked to imagine himself, free from the tragic flaws that so undermined him; ironically it was also, in many ways, what he was when he transformed himself into the writer who cooly and calculatedly assembled the often horrific ingredients of his superbly artful stories.

"The Murders in the Rue Morgue" opens with what is virtually an essay on the intellect:

> The mental features discoursed of as the analytical, are, in themselves, but little susceptible of analysis. We appreciate them only in their effects. . . . As the strong man exults in

> his physical ability, delighting in such exercises as call his muscles into action, so glories the analyst in that moral activity which *disentangles*.

Insight follows upon insight: "The analytical powers should not be confounded with simple ingenuity. . . . It will be found, in fact, that the ingenious are always fanciful, and the *truly* imaginative never otherwise than analytic." Only after setting this mental scene does the narrator introduce the instantly recognizable Monsieur C. Auguste Dupin:

> This young gentleman was of an excellent—indeed of an illustrious family, but, by a variety of untoward events, had been reduced to such poverty that the energy of his character succumbed beneath it. . . . [H]e managed, by means of rigorous economy, to procure the necessaries of life, without troubling himself about its superfluities. Books, indeed, were his sole luxuries, and in Paris these are easily obtained.

Dupin reads in the papers of "Extraordinary Murders" committed at the Rue Morgue in the Quartier St. Roche, and decides to investigate for himself. A reclusive mother and her daughter, Madame and Mademoiselle l'Espanaye, have been discovered dead after what appeared to have been a savage attack; yet all this had taken place in a room that remained locked. Witnesses who heard the screams of the women during the night attested to having heard two other voices—one a Frenchman, the other speaking a foreign language. The gendarme who heard them thought this foreign language was Spanish, another thought it was Italian, a Dutch witness thought it was French, a Spaniard thought it was English. The police soon arrested a bank clerk who had earlier that same day delivered a considerable sum of money to the women.

After examining the clues, Dupin discovers, by means of "ratiocination," the identity of the real culprit. The duly impressed narrator, the locked room, the deceptive clues, the police arrest of the wrong man—all these classic ingredients are already there in the very first detective story, whose final denouement proves every bit as extraordinary as the murders themselves.

Despite the success of Poe's stories, his financial and emotional state remained as precarious as ever. After earning ten dollars a week as assistant editor of *Burton's Gentleman's Magazine* in Philadelphia, in April 1841 he left to become editor of *Graham's Magazine*, but his lack of funds now forced him to consider the drastic step of giving up literary journalism altogether in order to provide for Virginia and her mother. In July he went so far as to apply for a post as a clerk in the Treasury Department at Washington, but was not accepted. Fortunately his editorship at *Graham's Magazine* soon proved a great success, and by the end of 1841 its circulation had increased to 25,000. He now managed to pay off his debts, and life at home with the Clemms was able to rise above the pressing miseries of unpaid bills and attendant poverty. Poe remained as deeply in love as ever with Virginia, who was now nineteen, and in the evenings after dinner Edgar would sometimes entertain Virginia and her mother by playing the flute, after which Virginia would sing, accompanying herself on the harp.

One evening in July 1842, while Virginia was singing to Poe and her mother, her voice suddenly failed and blood poured from her mouth. She had ruptured a blood vessel, and for a while her condition seemed so serious that it was thought she would die. She made a partial recovery, but there remained the threat of another hemorrhage, which might prove fatal. Virginia had always been frail, but it soon became clear that she was suffering from tuberculosis; she would eventually become bedridden. The strain of all this on the overworked Poe eventually led to another lapse into alcoholism, followed by bouts of erratic behavior and insomnia. He became afraid to fall asleep, on account of the horrific dreams that haunted him, declaring: "I believe that demons take advantage of the night to mislead the unwary—although, you know, I don't believe in them." Such ambiguity was by now typical of his life: his nightmares could appear more real than his working days. His fear of madness grew, and as a defense he cultivated his self-image as an "infallible ratiocinator." Modeling himself on his most sane creation, the superior-minded Monsieur Dupin, he began trying to solve crimes that he read about in the newspapers, and busied himself trying to decipher codes. Defiantly he would announce to anyone who would listen that there was no code in the world he could not crack. In May 1842, as a result of a minor misunderstanding, he simply walked out of *Graham's Magazine*.

The following year Poe's story "The Gold Bug" won a prize of one hundred dollars from the *Dollar Newspaper* of Philadelphia, and once again his fame spread throughout America. Poe's prizewinning story is permeated with the preoccupations that crowded his mind during this difficult period, and was intentionally sensational. This is a tale of hidden treasure in the form of a lost hoard of pirate's gold, and a secret message that will render its decoder rich beyond his dreams, all of which is set on an island off the Carolina coast. The hero of this often fantastic tale is William Legrand, "who had once been wealthy; but a series of misfortunes had reduced him to want. To avoid the mortification consequent upon his disasters, he left New Orleans, the city of his forefathers, and took up his residence at Sullivan's Island, near Charleston, South Carolina." The island is just three miles long and consists mostly of sand, a few miserable frame buildings, and some dense undergrowth; the narrator recounts how, "in the inmost recesses of this coppice, not far from the eastern or more remote end of the island, Legrand had built himself a small hut, which he occupied when I first, by mere accident, made his acquaintance." Poe's description of the South Carolina locale draws on his early period as a soldier in this region, providing an exotic and convincing background to a tale that is not always quite so convincing. Poe's ability to spin a good yarn, and to intrigue the reader, make up for the somewhat flimsy plot. Purely as an adventure story it certainly deserved to win the prize, though it is not Poe's finest literary work.

By now Poe had discovered a new talent to bring in money: he found that he had a gift for public speaking and began offering lectures on American literature. He had inherited from his parents a fine actor's voice, and he developed the ability to modulate and project this with the ease of a true professional. Poe's lectures on literature were informed with the understanding of a reflective practitioner; we can see from the criticism and essays that he published in various magazines that he had original views on such matters as "Poetry and Imagination," "Genius and Madness," and even "Intuition." His insights are seldom less than interesting: "Some of the most profound knowledge—perhaps all *very* profound knowledge—has originated from a highly stimulated imagination. Great intellects *guess* well. The laws of Kepler were, professedly, *guesses*." Poe read widely and was at home in science and philosophy as well as the more arcane reaches of literature. He also gave public readings of poetry, both his own and that of other well-known figures, such as his beloved English poets, including his favorite Byron and his new discovery Elizabeth Barrett Browning.

These readings were by all accounts both haunting and dramatic, and soon began pulling in crowds. Unfortunately there was only a limited circuit for such performances, and Poe had soon covered this. In 1844 he returned to New York, where he became an editor of the *Broadway Magazine*. By then he had published two more of his most characteristic horror stories, "The Pit and the Pendulum" and "The Black Cat."

"The Pit and the Pendulum" may not be entirely original—its basic ingredients are simply a combination of several different sources—but Poe's deeply felt rendering of the situation is utterly his own. The opening words mentally set the scene, plunging us directly into the world of the narrator:

> I was sick—sick unto death with that long agony; and when they at length unbound me, and I was permitted to sit, I felt that my senses were leaving me. The sentence, the dread sentence of death—was the last of distinct accentuation which reached my ears. After that, the sound of the inquisitorial

> voices seemed merged in one dreamy indeterminate hum.

The narrator has been sentenced to death by the Inquisition, which began in fifteenth-century Spain. Anyone suspected of heresy was hauled before its examiners, who were liable to extract confessions with tortures of fiendish cruelty before sentencing the hapless victim to death. In Poe's story we are not told of the religious crime of which the victim has been found guilty; all we know is the situation in which he finds himself. The tale concentrates on the method of execution.

As the narrator gradually regains consciousness, he remembers "the lips of the black-robed judges" which appeared "whiter than the sheet upon which I trace these words" as they sentenced him—and then he had swooned. Only gradually does he realize where he is now—in a dark dungeon, which he explores pacing out its length, soon making the alarming discovery that it appears to be growing smaller. In attempting to measure once more the proportions of his shrinking dungeon, he trips, falling flat on his face:

> In the confusion attending my fall, I did not apprehend a somewhat startling circumstance, which yet, in a few seconds afterward, while I still lay prostrate, arrested my attention. It was this—my chest rested upon the floor of the prison, but my lips and the upper portion of my head, although seemingly at a less elevation than the chin, touched nothing.

He appears to be at the very brink of a chasm. He succeeds in dislodging a fragment from the wall and hears it falling down into the abyss, reverberating against the sides of the pit before eventually, far, far below, it plunges into water.

Some time later he looks up toward the ceiling thirty or forty feet above him, where "a very singular figure riveted my attention. It was the painted figure of Time as he is commonly represented, save that, in lieu of a scythe, he held what, at a casual glance, I supposed to be the pictured image of a huge pendulum." He realizes that the pendulum is swinging, then he notices that its swing is getting wider, and "as a natural consequence, its velocity was also much greater." Only then does he notice that the pendulum is descending toward him, whereupon he makes out that its lower edge is a blade "evidently as keen as that of a razor."

The narrator finds himself between the pit and the descending pendulum. In Poe's telling, the sheer terror of the situation is rendered all too real, yet such an archetypal situation is also inevitably open to allegorical and psychological interpretation. The pendulum seems to be in the hands of Father Time; the pit, the deep abyss below, is the hell of all our worst fears, and also the inevitable end that awaits us all. Death and the unconscious, the inevitable shrinking of time—these universal images are concentrated into a tale that is nothing less than a nightmare. Yet like a nightmare, we will also awaken from it. Poe hints at this when the narrator describes at the outset the lips of the judges being "whiter than the sheet upon which I trace these words." This is presented as no imaginary tale, no fantasy—the narrator will somehow survive, just as we eventually wake from a nightmare. This adds to both the verisimilitude of the tale (this is the situation of all true nightmares, from which we awake) and also the suspense (how can the narrator possibly escape?).

Claustrophobia, infantile terror of the dark and of the unknown that it masks—several critics have pointed out the similarity of the narrator's predicament and that of the child within the womb, as well as the knife that cuts it out of the womb when a cesarean section is carried out. Such overly psychological interpretations often appear farfetched, but there is no denying the utterly primal fears described and evoked by Poe in this particular tale, which may indeed relate to his earliest prenatal consciousness. Other clues reinforce this possible interpretation—such as the cell growing smaller (the child growing in the womb), the hiss of the descending pendulum as it slices through the air (mimicking the rustle of breath in the regularly expanding and contracting lungs above the womb), and so forth. But such elements are scattered through the text, and many more elements do not support such a precise psychological reading. So should it be dismissed? Poe may well have included such references unconsciously, for his writing was often highly attuned to his unconscious feelings, and these indications certainly have their effect on the reader, if only in their reinforcement of the horror. There is no denying that there is something primal about the life and death forces at work in Poe's telling of "The Pit and the Pendulum"; and as such, reading it can be an inexplicably intense and profound experience, which remains memorable for all its apparent simplicity. The unraveling of the simple plot may not be a resolution of great literature, but the situation itself remains an unforgettable image. We have never been in such an Inquisition dungeon, yet when reading Poe's words we somehow seem to recognize the predicament. Was this from a nightmare, or did it arise from something that predated our sleeping dreams—our original quasi-conscious experience?

"The Black Cat" inhabits a similar territory of almost unspeakable horror. The opening lines betray the narrator's ambivalence about what he is about to reveal—an ambivalence which was almost certainly felt by Poe too, for this was a brave story fraught with self-revelation:

> For the most wild, yet homely narrative which I am about to pen, I neither expect nor solicit belief. Mad indeed would I be to expect it, in a case where my very senses reject their own evidence. Yet mad I am not. . . .

As we shall see, this last denial is particularly significant.

Poe's tale is simple enough, centering on the animal of the title, but in many ways it is Poe's most candidly autobiographical tale. The narrator is an apparently likable fellow:

> From my infancy I was noted for the docility and humanity of my disposition. My tenderness of heart was even so conspicuous as to make me the jest of my companions. I was very fond of animals. . . .

In later life he married and "was happy to find in my wife a disposition not uncongenial to my own." They had a family pet, a cat, which "was a remarkably large and beautiful animal, entirely black, and sagacious to an astonishing degree." Having set this cozy domestic scene, Poe subtly hints at what is to come. "In speaking of [the cat's] intelligence, my wife, who at heart was not a little tinctured with superstition, made frequent allusion to the ancient popular notion which regarded all black cats as witches in disguise."

Eventually the narrator succumbs to "the Fiend Intemperance," and when drunk he becomes a sadistic monster. One night after he returns home "much intoxicated, from one of my haunts about town," he senses that the cat is avoiding him; annoyed at this, he siezes the animal, which bites him. "The fury of a demon instantly possessed me. I knew myself no longer. My original soul seemed, at once, to take its flight from my body. . . . I took from my waistcoat-pocket a pen-knife, opened it, grasped the poor beast by the throat, and deliberately cut one of its eyes from the socket."

Edgar Allan Poe had arrived at the notion of Dr. Jekyll and Mr. Hyde almost half a century before Robert Louis Stevenson wrote his classic story of split personality, and Poe more than manages to convey the profound anguish experienced by such a personality. Having described how he cut out the cat's eye, the narrator cried out: "I blush, I burn, I shudder, while I pen the damnable atrocity."

But this tale is prompted by much more than Poe's self-disgust and horror at his own uncontrolled drunken behavior. Beneath it lies his fear of succumbing to madness and the unspeakable acts that his disturbed mind may well have suggested to him, may even have prompted him to consider acting upon. Poe loved his invalid young wife, now reduced to her bed and appearing more than ever like the child he had married; yet she was a burden to him, and her illness drove him to despair and drink. Poe was honest enough to confront his fears and attempt to examine them—perhaps even exorcise them—in this painful story, which is at once deeply personal and yet has the timeless rounded plot of a fairy tale. "Of my own thoughts it is folly to speak," exclaims the narrator near the end—but by then Poe has made us fully aware of the deep contradictory forces that assail him. This very admission leads the tale toward the poetic justice of its conclusion, which has the tragic inevitability of ancient myth.

During his stay in New York, Poe once more turned to journalism to bring in money. He published a regular column for *Godey's Lady's Book* entitled "Literati," in which he satirized a number of contemporary New York writers. Poe's work, and his behavior, had earned him a number of enemies among the New York literati: some were jealous of his talent, others were antagonized by the insulting opinions to which Poe gave voice when he was drunk. As a result, his stories were frequently rejected by local magazines, and his applications for permanent positions regularly suffered a similar fate. Poe's satirical column gave him the chance to settle a few old scores, and this he did with glee, frequently descending to plain invective. The Nantucket-born writer Charles T. Briggs was made a laughingstock: "Mr. Briggs has never composed in his life three consecutive sentences of grammatical English. He is grossly uneducated." The critic Lewis Gaylord Clark was described as being "noticeable for nothing in the world except for the markedness by which he is noticeable for nothing." Such remarks inevitably led to slanging matches and occasional fisticuffs in the literary waterholes; counterattacks, lawsuits, and countersuits soon followed.

All this may have been a distraction, but it would lead Poe to write one of his best-known pieces—"The Cask of Amontillado," a tale of revenge. This is narrated by Montresor, whose opening words come straight to the point: "The thousand injuries of Fortunato I had borne as best I could, but when he ventured upon insult I vowed revenge." Montresor disguises his feelings, pretending that he is still a friend of Fortunato, and "one evening during the supreme madness of the carnival season I encountered my friend. He accosted me with excessive warmth, for he had been drinking much." Fortunato "prided himself on his connoisseurship of wine," and Montresor takes him back home, finally luring Fortunato down into the family vaults where he keeps a cask of Amontillado wine. The vaults are suitably gloomy and contain the bones of Montresor's enemies as well as the cask.

Montresor's revenge bears a resemblance to the action of "The Black Cat" and other stories; Poe's work contains several recurrent themes which have deep psychological resonances. "The Cask of Amontillado" is certainly a psychological working out of what he would have liked to do to Briggs, Clark, or indeed any of his several enemies. But on a deeper level this is also another forerunner of the Jekyll and Hyde theme. Montresor ("my treasure") is the sober rational side of Poe, while Fortunato ("fortune" or "fate") is the alcoholic, self-destructive element with which he is cursed. One wished to imprison the other, to kill him, to eliminate the chaos he felt to be overwhelming him. It is Poe's profound involvement in such tales that gives an added intensity to their telling.

The same is true of Poe's poetry, which often has an ethereal, haunting quality. This is emphasized by repetition and resonance. Nowhere is this more evident than in his poem "Ulalume," whose very title evokes its own ethereal, essentially unknowable quality, much like music. This mood is established in the opening lines:

The skies they were ashen and sober;
  The leaves they were crisped and sere—
  The leaves they were withering and sere;
It was night in the lonesome October
  Of my most immemorial year . . .

Although "Ulalume" may be described as a love poem, Poe's essential intention was the evocation of a soul-scape. The same may be said of most of his more successful poems, especially the one with which his name will forever be associated, "The Raven," whose opening lines have become an indelible part of the English language:

Once upon a midnight dreary, while I pondered, weak and weary,
  Over many a quaint and curious volume of forgotten lore—
  While I nodded, nearly napping, suddenly there came a tapping,
  As of some one gently rapping, rapping at my chamber door.

"'Tis some visitor," I muttered, "tapping at my chamber door—
Only this and nothing more."

This poem was dedicated to Elizabeth Barrett Browning—whom Poe had never met, but with whom he had corresponded, generously and effusively addressing her as "the greatest, most glorious of her sex" (much to her Victorian embarrassment). Before writing "The Raven," Poe had rapturously read Mrs. Browning's recent poem "Lady Geraldine's Courtship," and there is more than a passing resemblance between certain lines in the two poems, as can be seen in the following line from Mrs. Browning:

"With a murmurous stir uncertain in the air the purple curtain"

and:

"And the silken sad uncertain rustling of each purple curtain,"

Poe's is of course the latter. Yet apart from such all too obvious resemblances, "The Raven" remains utterly characteristic of Poe, and as such original. Even more original was Poe's later decision to let his readers in on the secret of how he composed his masterpiece. Few poets before had dared to describe how they came to write poetry—indeed, most had preferred to remain blissfully unaware of the exact methods used by the poetic muse to inspire the poet, while others who had pondered this problem had preferred to keep their findings to themselves, unwilling to divulge the magic of creation. Poe, virtually alone among poets, was willing to dispel this age-old mystery which had defied both self-analysis and psychology.

In his essay "The Philosophy of Composition," Poe claimed that before writing "The Raven" he set about calculating all aspects of the poem, which were chosen for optimum effect. This included even the poem's length, "for it is clear that the brevity must be in direct ratio of the intensity of the intended effect." This led him to conclude "what I conceived the proper *length* for my intended poem—a length of about one hundred lines." He adds triumphantly: "It is, in fact, a hundred and eight." In the course of this argument he points out that in general "a certain degree of duration is absolutely requisite for the production of any effect at all." "The Raven" was thus written according to a strict mathematical formula, by means of a series of calculated logical operations: "throughout the construction I kept steadily in view the design of rendering the work *universally* appreciable." He then goes on to describe the logical thought process by which he chose the subject of his great poem, and how "very naturally, a parrot, in the first instance, suggested itself." At this stage it becomes clear that Poe is being ironic: "The Raven" was far from being a humorous poem, but its author was always capable of making a joke at his own expense. For all his intensity and self-revelation, which often appears so unwitting and naive, Poe remained very much a sophisticated artist, well aware of what he was doing. Any analysis of Poe's work—from literary criticism to depth psychology—must always bear this in mind.

There is in fact good reason for Poe's little joke about the conception and writing of "The

Raven." Together with the joke at the reader's expense, and at his own expense, he wished to make a joke at the expense of the poem—which so captured the popular imagination that it was already becoming a cliché in his own lifetime. Poe had hardly intended this, but he had sufficient critical acumen to recognize what was happening to this work that the public so loved to hear him recite. In his essay "The Philosophy of Composition" he wished to defend himself against the charge of having composed a hackneyed work—and what better way to do this than to produce a spoof claim that he had cynically calculated all the ingredients necessary for a popular hit?

And yet. There is no doubt that Poe *did* set down a plan for "The Raven" before writing it—the poem has the plot and tone of one of his short stories, and gains all the more from its narrative element and its subtle shifts of modulation. Once again the narrative is simple enough in outline. The narrator, a mourning lover, is distracted by the tapping of the Raven at his chamber door. The Raven enters, the poet questions the bird—asking the Raven its name, asking if he will ever be able to forget his lost love Lenore, whether he will one day find her in heaven? And in answer to each of his questions he receives the same reply: "Quoth the Raven, 'Nevermore.'" Finally he is reduced to begging the Raven to go away:

> "Leave my loneliness unbroken!—quit the bust above my door!
> Take thy beak from out my heart, and take thy form from off my door!"
> Quoth the Raven, "Nevermore."

The poem's final verse begins:

> And the Raven, never flitting, still is sitting, still is sitting
> On the pallid bust of Pallas just above my chamber door;
> And his eyes have all the seeming of a demon's that is dreaming . . .

Once more, Poe was trying to exorcise his fears. In 1846, together with Virginia and her mother, he moved to a cottage in the woods at Fordham, thirteen miles outside New York City. It had been clear for some time that Virginia was dying, and this had been preying on Poe's mind while he had been composing "The Raven." The black bird of pain, suffering, and evil would never "take thy beak from out my heart." After having been nursed through the last stages of her illness by her husband, Virginia finally died on January 30, 1847, at the age of twenty-four.

Poe was distraught, and was soon battling again with his alcoholism. When he was sober, the celebrated author of "The Raven" cut an enigmatic, distinctly romantic figure, which proved attractive to a number of motherly middle-aged women who sought to look after him (not always in an entirely motherly fashion). He needed the support of women, and after the death of his wife he became embroiled in several intense affairs, some of the women providing him with much-needed money as well as emotional support. Such affairs were for the most part platonic, as far as it is possible to tell, but they inspired Poe to write a stream of love poems.

Typical of these are the poems he wrote to Marie Louise Shew. Unlike so many of Poe's "muses," she was not a literary lady but had some medical expertise. Poe had been befriended by Mrs. Shew some time before Virginia's death, and she had helped Mrs. Clemm to look after the ailing wife and her distraught husband. (Virginia's mother was more than tolerant of the women who positively buzzed around Poe at this time; she knew that Virginia would die and wanted only the best for her beloved son-in-law. Even Virginia appears to have encouraged some of these friendships, which she felt sure would bring Poe the comfort and protection he needed when she was gone.) So as Poe tended to Virginia, Mrs. Shew tended to Poe, and he wrote her such lines as:

> Not long ago, the writer of these lines,
> In the mad pride of intellectuality,
> Maintained "the power of words"—denied
>   that ever
> A thought arose within the human brain
> Beyond the utterance of the human tongue:

And now, as if in mockery of that boast,
Two words—two foreign soft disyllables—
. . . I see . . .
Amid empurpled vapors, far away
To where the prospect terminates—*thee only*.

Some of his other love poems are less straightforward, such as this poem which is "For Annie" and is about Virginia's death as well as his love for Annie, and hints at a morbid side to Poe's sexuality:

Thank Heaven! the crisis—
  The danger is past,
And the lingering illness
  Is over at last—
And the fever called "Living"
  Is conquered at last . . .
. . .
And I lie so composedly,
  Now in my bed,
(Knowing her love,)
  That you fancy me dead . . .
That you shudder to look at me,
  Thinking me dead:—

But while he repeats again and again how he resembles the dead, and she thinks of him as dead, his "heart . . . glows with the light of my love of my Annie."

Love and death remained inseparably linked in Poe's mind, from the death of his mother when he was almost three years old, to the very end of his life when he wrote his extraordinary poem "To My Mother." Here the particular figure of his mother becomes dissolved into an archetypal Mother who is addressed as

> You who are more than mother unto me,
> And fill my heart of hearts, where Death installed you
> In setting my Virginia's spirit free.

Needless to say, such poems have led to all manner of psychological interpretation. On the surface this "mother" seems not to be his real dead mother but instead Mrs. Clemm, "mother of the one I loved so dearly." But otherworldly aspects ascribed to her, such as "setting my Virginia's spirit free," would seem to suggest a more archetypal figure that haunted Poe's mind.

After Virginia's death, Mrs. Shew took on the role of Poe's love, but she soon found his companionship too demanding and difficult. She was expected to be his muse, his mother, his medical nurse, his (platonic) lover, and his literary soul mate—an impossible role for any woman, especially one who had no real interest in literature. No longer capable of devoting herself to Poe, she left him and devoted herself to religion instead.

Poe now found himself virtually besieged by enamored middle-aged women, several of whom he would fall briefly in love with (often more than one at a time). Eventually he fell more deeply in love with Sarah Helen Whitman, of Providence, Rhode Island, a woman of some intelligence and sensibility. Despite this, she was hardly suitable for Poe, being a prim spiritualist who disapproved of alcohol yet was herself secretly addicted to ether; on the other hand, she had enough money to support him, being both a property owner and heiress to a modest fortune. After an exchange of letters and poems, Poe traveled to see Mrs. Whitman. Despite the fact that he arrived in Providence in a somewhat hysterical state, owing to his nerves and his alcoholism, Mrs. Whitman agreed to marry Poe, and they became engaged—on the condition that Poe indulged in no further "erratic behavior." Inevitably Mrs. Whitman was soon tipped off about Poe's covert visits to local bars, and the engagement was called off.

Poe now traveled to Boston, where a few weeks later he tried to commit suicide by drinking laudanum, though this botched attempt was actually intended to impress another woman with whom he had now become infatuated. Poe's life was rapidly spiraling out of control.

Astonishingly, he had recently produced a work of considerable learning and erudition, on science and philosophy. This was utterly different from anything he had produced before in the course of his varied career, and was certainly his most ambitious work. It was called *Eureka: An Essay on the Material and Spiritual Universe*, and appears to have been inspired by his reading of the first volume of the multivolume *Cosmos* by Alexander von Humboldt, the great German naturalist and explorer of South America. Von

Humboldt had, in his own words, been inspired by "the crazy notion to depict in a single work the entire material universe, all that we know of the phenomena of heaven and earth, from the nebulae of stars to the geography of mosses and granite rocks—and in a vivid style that will stimulate and elicit feeling."

Poe's aim was similarly grandiose, though this ambition would manifest itself in more poetic brevity. In the Preface of *Eureka*, Poe declares, "I offer this Book of Truths, not in its character of Truth-Teller, but for the Beauty that abounds in its Truth. . . . Nevertheless, it is as a Poem only that I wish this work to be judged after I am dead." At the outset he declares his intention to view the universe as a unity—illustrating what this means and what he hoped to gain by doing so: "He who from the top of Etna casts his eyes leisurely around is affected chiefly by the extent and diversity of the scene. Only by a rapid whirling on his heel could he hope to comprehend the panorama in the sublimity of its oneness." Only in this way will it be possible to explain the entire workings of the universe, for

"In the Original Unity of the First Thing lies the Secondary Cause of All Things."

In the early pages of *Eureka*, Poe refers to a veritable plethora of figures, ranging from Euclid and Aristotle through Bacon, Kepler, Newton, Laplace, Leibniz, and Hume, even including Jean-François Champollion (who had recently deciphered the hieroglyphs of ancient Egypt). If nothing else, this indicates the breadth of his reading, to say nothing of his ambition, and the reader is soon eagerly anticipating the author's pratfalls. It quickly becomes evident that Poe is no scientist and has little specialist understanding of science and philosophy; yet it becomes equally clear that his imagination in this sphere remains of the highest originality and knows no bounds. With the innocence of the newcomer, he raises a number of striking and perceptive points and is willing to question the wisdom of even the greatest contemporary philosophers, such as John Stuart Mill.

Poe also has the temerity to question the cornerstone of his contemporary science: "The great mind of Newton, while boldly grasping the Law [of Gravity] itself shrank from the principle of the Law." Poe points out that "while all men have admitted *some* principle as existing behind the Law of Gravity, no attempt has been yet made to point out what this principle in particular is." In other words, what lies behind the laws that govern the workings of the universe? Why should they be the way they are, and not some other way? Only in the late twentieth century would scientists seriously begin to tackle such questions.

More than 150 years after the publication of *Eureka*, the well-known British astronomer Sir Patrick Moore noted that "when [Poe] turns to cosmology he introduces concepts which are well ahead of their time." Among these is the idea of cosmological expansion. Poe clearly states that "the universe of stars is the result of radiation from that center." He also speculates that our galaxy must have a vast central sun, going on to ask, why "do we not *see* this vast central sun? At least equal in mass to one hundred million suns such as ours . . . it must be non-luminous as are our planets." As Moore points out: "Today we have strong evidence of a super-massive black hole at the galactic centre." Poe also suggested that "in all probability" revolving around the sun there were "several more [planets] of which as yet we know nothing," going on to speculate that the Milky Way was but one of many such galaxies. And he proposed an ingenious explanation for why it is dark at night—because light from distant galaxies has yet to reach us.

On the other hand, many critics have dismissed Poe's *Eureka* as no better than the ramblings of a disordered mind, one going so far as to describe it as "little more than a compendium of nonsense, its metaphysical darkness illuminated only by the occasional spark of inspired (or lucky) guesswork." Even Moore is forced to concede that it is "frankly obscure in places," and that in many passages Poe "may be accused of playing with words."

In Poe's own estimation, *Eureka* was his finest work, the masterpiece on which he would "be judged after I am dead." In fairness it is worth pointing out that by this stage in Poe's life his judgment had been severely eroded by alcoholism and nervous disorders. Yet even under the best of circumstances, great artists are seldom the best judges of their own work. The ever-sober Nabokov, for instance, considered the hopelessly self-indulgent *Ada* to be his crowning masterwork; and the young genius Rimbaud, whose work transformed French literature, gave up writing poetry in his early twenties and from then on regarded all his work as a juvenile aberration.

So what was *Eureka*? A masterpiece, or simply nonsense, or possibly a very rare blend of both? Whichever it is, *Eureka* undeniably illustrates Poe's deep and lasting interest in science and emphasizes an element of his character that is implicit in so much of his writing. Although he recognized the power of the imagination, he always saw himself as a man of reason. His wildest fantasies were invariably grounded in fact, science, or "ratiocination." It is this self-conception that makes Poe's work so convincing, lending it a constant air of plausibility.

Alas, the same cannot be said of his life, especially by this late stage. In January 1849 Poe found himself in New York once more; he was forty years old and desperate to find a backer for a new magazine he wished to edit. After months of sporadic effort he finally managed to interest an Illinois newspaper owner named Edward Paterson. In June Poe set out from New York for Richmond, Virginia, intending to raise more money and arrange advance publicity for his magazine. Instead, as we have seen, he ended up in Philadelphia in a state of raving intoxication.

Two weeks later he finally reached Richmond, where he encountered his former childhood sweetheart Sarah Elmira Royster, who twenty years previously had been unwilling to await his return from the University of Virginia. She was now Mrs. Shelton, and a widow. They soon fell for each other again and decided to marry; there followed some months of comparative stability in Poe's life. Despite this, he appears to have had premonitions of his own death. He had already appointed his "friend" the Reverend Rufus W. Griswold, a Baptist clergyman, as his literary executor. Poe and Griswold had known each other since 1841, when they had collaborated on a literary project. During this period Poe had briefly quarreled with Griswold, yet they had soon resumed their friendship. But unknown to Poe, Griswold had never forgotten their falling out, nor had he forgiven Poe. Secretly Griswold had continued to harbor a deep grudge against Poe, which had grown ever deeper as he watched Poe's increasing fame and increasingly wayward behavior.

In September 1849 Poe left for New York, which he never reached, instead dying in a hospital in Baltimore after having been found unconscious drunk in the street outside a bar. On October 9 he was buried in the Presbyterian cemetery at Fayette and Green Streets in Baltimore. Some years later his body was reburied in the southeastern corner of the cemetery beside those of his wife Virginia and her mother.

Afterword

All that remained now was for Griswold to do his worst, and he certainly went to some pains to achieve this in his attempt to blacken Poe's name forever. News of Poe's death quickly spread along the telegraph wires of the eastern seaboard, and on the very day of Poe's funeral Griswold published a notice in the *New York Tribune* announcing Poe's demise, which included the following: "This announcement will startle many, but few will be grieved by it. The poet was known personally, or by reputation in all this country . . . but he had few or no friends and the regrets for his death will be [mainly for the loss to] literary art." Griswold went on to outline Poe's life, delighting in describing Poe's poverty and disgrace as well as a particular occasion when "a tattered frock coat concealed the absence of a shirt, and the ruins of boots disclosed more than the want of stockings." His description of how Poe normally appeared was little better: "He was at all times a dreamer—dwelling in ideal realms—in heaven or hell—peopled with the creatures and the accidents of his brain. He walked the streets, in madness or melancholy, with lips moving in indistinct curses."

Although to begin with Griswold tried to appear balanced and fair by praising Poe's purely literary abilities, he could not help adding that Poe "himself dissolved the spell, and brought his hearers back to common and base existence, by vulgar fancies or exhibitions of the ignoble passions." As Poe's literary executor, Griswold was duty bound to arrange for the posthumous publication of Poe's collected works, but he made sure that this was prefaced by his own forty-page "Memoir," in which he perpetrated further inaccuracies.

Even before Poe died, several of his works had crossed the Atlantic. His stories and poems became well known in England, and in 1847 a French translation of "The Black Cat" was published in the Paris magazine *La Démocratie Pacifique.* This proved so popular that it was soon followed by "The Gold Bug" and other works. These were read by the great French poet Charles Baudelaire, who immediately recognized in Poe a kindred spirit. Baudelaire too suffered from alcoholism, constant lack of money, and the contempt of his less talented literary peers because of the sensational subject of his works. Baudelaire quickly became so obsessed with Poe that he relearned English in order to translate as many of Poe's works as he could find. He even began seeking out details of Poe's life, and in 1852 published a long article about the American. Baudelaire's memoir of Poe was a suitable counterbalance to Griswold's, and was almost equally biased—though in the opposite direction. The unhappy Baudelaire heavily identified himself with Poe; he too saw himself as a doomed figure, and the resulting memoir borders on hagiography.

> The life of Poe, his morals, his manners, his physical being, all that constituted his personal surroundings, appear as at once gloomy and brilliant. His person, singularly entrancing, was like his works, marked with an indefinable stamp of melancholy. Moreover, he was remarkably well endowed in all aspects. . . . There are some points relative to Poe upon which there is a unanimous agreement, for example his high natural distinction, his eloquence and his beauty. . . .

And so on, for more than twenty pages—which, despite such exaggeration, make moving reading in light of the miserable lives lived by both the author and his subject. By now Baudelaire had read Griswold's infamous "Memoir," and took this occasion to set the record straight. Griswold was duly castigated as a "pedagogic vampire" of the "dullest unintelligence" belonging to the "hypocritical trading class."

Baudelaire was too much a habitual artist to confine himself to a purely literal translation of Poe's work, and his renderings of Poe into French rank alongside some of his finest original work (often being of a similar originality). Indeed, Baudelaire's translation of the opening page of "The Fall of the House of Usher" has been called one of the finest French prose poems of its time.

This was just the beginning, and soon Poe's work was being translated throughout the world. In America he became acknowledged as one of the greatest writers of the nineteenth century, alongside Walt Whitman and Herman Melville. The popular nature of his work ensured his continuing popularity, though it also prompted many academic critics to belittle Poe. Only in France was he regarded as a high artist, a pioneer of literary genres, and an embodiment of Romantic genius. This tradition would continue well into the twentieth century, with that most intellectual of French poets Paul Valéry going so far as to claim: "He is absolutely the only writer who had the intuition to link literature and the mind." Such hyperbole does neither Poe nor Valéry any good. On the other hand, it was Valéry who grasped the central idea of *Eureka*, which he expressed as: "In the beginning was the fable. It will be there always." But as with so many intellectuals, Valéry had his blind spot where humor was concerned; he appears to have taken Poe's "Philosophy of Composition" in all seriousness, completely overlooking its comic element.

Understood, or misunderstood, Poe would remain over the years as popular and widely read as ever. Several of his stories have achieved the accolade of being transmogrified into bad Hollywood movies bearing little relation to the original. Yet there is something archetypal in his work which manages to survive even this. Several of his poems—most notably "The Raven"—have achieved the ultimate distinction of becoming a part of American literary consciousness. Whether it is regarded as great literature or no, some of Poe's lines now have the status attained only by Shakespeare, popular music, and cinematic wisecracks—they are so well known that they have become part of the language:

> Once upon a midnight dreary, while I pondered weak and weary . . .

From Poe's Writings

One of the opening verses of "The Raven":

And the silken sad uncertain rustling of each purple curtain
Thrilled me—filled me with fantastic terrors never felt before;
So that now, to still the beating of my heart, I stood repeating:
"'Tis some visitor entreating entrance at my chamber door—
Some late visitor entreating entrance at my chamber door;
That it is and nothing more."

Later he addresses the raven, who gives his celebrated reply:

"Prophet!" said I, "thing of evil!—prophet still, if bird or devil!
By that heaven that bends above us—by that God we both adore—
Tell this soul with sorrow laden if, within the distant Aidenn,
It shall clasp a sainted maiden whom the angels name Lenore—
Clasp a rare and radiant maiden whom the angels name Lenore."
Quoth the Raven, "Nevermore."

"Be that word our sign of parting, bird or fiend!" I shrieked, upstarting—
"Get thee back into the tempest and the Night's Plutonian shore!
Leave no black plume as a token of that lie thy soul hath spoken!
Leave my loneliness unbroken!—quit the bust above my door!

Take thy beak from out my heart, and take thy
form from off my door!"
Quoth the Raven, "Nevermore."

The opening lines of Poe's acrostic poem "A Valentine," to Frances Sargent Osgood, in which her name is spelt out in the first letter of the first line, second letter of the second line, and so on.

For her this rhyme is penned, whose luminous eyes,
Brightly expressive of the twins of Leda,
Shall find her own sweet name, that, nestling lies
Upon the page, enwrapped from every reader.
Search narrowly the lines!—they hold a treasure
Divine—a talisman—an amulet
That must be worn *at heart*. Search well the measure . . .

The famous opening of "The Fall of the House of Usher," which the French poet Baudelaire would later "adapt" into one of the finest prose poems in the French language:

Son coeur est un luth suspendu;
Sitôt qu'on le touche il résonne.
(*His heart is a suspended lute;*
As soon as it is touched it resounds.)
—De Béranger

During the whole of a dull, dark, and soundless day in the autumn of the year, when the clouds hung oppressively low in the heavens, I had been passing alone, on horseback, through a singularly dreary tract of country, and at length found myself, as the shades of the evening drew on, within view of the melancholy House of Usher. I know not how it was—but, with the first glimpse of the building, a sense of insufferable gloom pervaded my spirit. I say insufferable; for the feeling was unrelieved by any of that half-pleasurable, because poetic, sentiment with which the mind usually receives even the sternest natural images of the desolate or terrible. I looked upon the scene before me—upon the mere house, and the simple landscape features of the domain—upon the bleak walls—upon the vacant eye-like windows—upon a few rank sedges—and upon a few white trunks of decayed trees—with an utter depression of soul which I can compare to no earthly sensation more properly than to the after-dream of the reveller upon opium—the bitter lapse into every-day life—the hideous dropping off of the veil. There was an iciness, a sinking, a sickening of the heart—an unredeemed dreariness of thought which no goading of the imagination could torture into aught of the sublime. What was it—I paused to think—what was it that so unnerved me in the contemplation of the House of Usher? It was a mystery all insoluble; nor could I grapple with the shadowy fancies that crowded upon me as I pondered.

From his essay "The Poetic Principle":

I would define, in brief, the Poetry of words as *The Rhythmical Creation of Beauty.* Its sole arbiter is Taste. With the Intellect or with the Conscience, it has only collateral relations. Unless incidentally, it has no concern whatever either with Duty or with Truth.

A few words, however, in explanation. *That* pleasure which is at once the most pure, the most elevating, and the most intense, is derived, I maintain, from the contemplation of the Beautiful. In the contemplation of Beauty we alone find it possible to attain that pleasurable elevation, or excitement, *of the soul*, which we recognize as the Poetic Sentiment, and which is so easily distinguished from Truth, which is the satisfaction of the Reason, or from Passion, which is the excitement of the Heart.

Poe's Chief Works

Poe's short stories and poems were for the most part published separately in magazines and journals before being collected and published in book form. I have listed the titles of his better-known stories and poems rather than his collections, which sometimes overlapped.

"Tamerlane" (1827)†
"Al Aaraaf" (1829)†
"MS. Found in a Bottle" (1833)†
"The Unparalleled Adventure of One Hans Pfaall" (1935)†
"Ligeia" (1838)*†

*major works
†discussed in text

"The Narrative of Arthur Gordon Pym of Nantucket" (1838)†
"The Fall of the House of Usher" (1839)*†
"The Murders in the Rue Morgue" (1841)*†
"The Gold Bug" (1843)†
"The Black Cat" (1843)*†
"The Pit and the Pendulum" (1843)*†
"The Raven" (1845)*†
"The Cask of Amontillado" (1846)†
"Ulalume" (1847)†
Eureka (1848)*†
"For Annie" (1849)†
"To My Mother" (1849)†

Chronology of Poe's Life and Times

1809	Edgar Poe born in Boston on January 19, son of actors David and Elizabeth Arnold Poe.
1810	Father abandons family.
1811	Death of Poe's mother; taken into household of John Allen, a Richmond merchant.
1815	Taken with Allen and family to Scotland and England.
1820	Returns with Allens to America.
1826	Attends University of Virginia for one year.

1827	To Boston, where he publishes *Tamerlane and Other Poems*. Enlists in army under name Edgar A. Perry.
1829	January: promoted to regimental sergeant-major. April: obtains discharge from army. August: lives in Baltimore with his aunt, Maria Clemm, and her young daughter Virginia.
1830	Enters U.S. Military Academy at West Point.
1831	January: court-martialed and dismissed from West Point. March: publication of *Poems*. November: arrested for debt; paid off two months later by John Allen, the last payment he will make to Poe.
1833	Poe's short story "MS. Found in a Bottle" wins fifty-dollar short-story prize.
1834	His wealthy guardian John Allen dies, leaving nothing to Poe in his will.
1835	Writes "The Unparalleled Adventure of One Hans Pfaall," now widely accepted as the first work of science fiction. May: begins writing regular contributions and reviews for the *Southern Literary*

Messenger, soon obtaining the post of assistant editor from its owner Thomas White. September: dismissed from *Southern Literary Messenger* for "unreliability." October: reinstated as editor of *Southern Literary Messenger*.

1836 May: marries his cousin Virginia Clemm, who is now thirteen years old.

1837 January: resigns as editor of the *Southern Literary Messenger*, moves to New York in February. April: panic on New York stock market leads to closure of many magazines as depression spreads through U.S. Mrs. Clemm forced to take in boarders.

1838 Publication in book form of *The Narrative of Arthur Gordon Pym of Nantucket*. Moves to Philadelphia.

1840 *Tales of the Grotesque and Arabesque* published in Philadelphia.

1841 Unsuccessful attempt to obtain post as clerk in Treasury Department, Washington. In spring Poe first meets the

	anthologist Dr. Rufus Wilmot Griswold, and in June writes a favorable review of his *Poets and Poetry of America*.
1842	Poe's wife Virginia suffers serious hemorrhage.
1843	Publication of "The Gold Bug" brings public renown. *The Prose Romances of Edgar A. Poe* published in Philadelphia.
1844	First publication of "The Raven" establishes Poe as a national literary figure.
1845	Meets poet Frances Sargent Osgood, who begins to pursue him; her writings about Poe cause a scandal. Publication of *The Raven and Other Poems*.
1846	May: moves to cottage at Fordham, New York. Writes "Literati of New York" sketches, which result in libel action.
1847	January: his wife Virginia dies of pulmonary consumption at the age of twenty-four. Anonymous publication of "Ulalume"
1848	In Providence, Rhode Island, he becomes briefly engaged to the poet Sarah Helen

Whitman. Consequent platonic entanglements with several women. May: publication of *Eureka: A Prose Poem*, his quasi-scientific metaphysical explanation of the universe.

1849 Arrives in Philadelphia in state of drunken delirium. Recovers, travels to Richmond, and plans to marry Sarah Elmira Royster. September: leaves Richmond for New York. October 3: found unconscious in a street in Baltimore. October 7: dies at Washington College Hospital, Baltimore, leaving Griswold as his literary executor.

Recommended Reading

Charles Baudelaire, *The Painters of Modern Life and Other Essays* (Phaidon Press, 1995). Well worth searching out, this volume, or indeed any full edition of the French poet's essays, includes his studies on Poe. These are in many ways wildly biased toward his hero, and as such can be heartening. At the same time Baudelaire's empathy with his "American brother" leads to many perceptive insights into what Poe was doing and what he wished to achieve.

Marie Bonaparte, *The Life and Works of Edgar Allan Poe: A Psychoanalytic Interpretation* (Anglobooks, 1952). The great in-depth psychoanalytic study of Poe and his works by the celebrated French pupil of Freud. Poe's work is particularly open to this kind of interpretation, and

Bonaparte brings all her skills and imagination to the task. Many of her conclusions may appear farfetched or exaggerated, but there is no denying the compelling ingenuity of some of her insightful findings. The book is designed to make you think, and fully succeeds.

The Cambridge Companion to Edgar Allan Poe (New York, 2002). An orthodox approach to Poe, though given the nature of the subject and his work these essays are far from dull. Topics range from "Poe's Feminine Ideal" to "Poe and Popular Culture," from "Poe, Sensationalism and Slavery" to "One-Man Modernist." The collection is edited by Poe scholar Kevin J. Hayes, whose wife Myung-Sook Hayes has produced an ingenious diagram of the opening sentence of "The Fall of the House of Usher."

Collected Works of Edgar Allan Poe (Greystone Press, 1980). These volumes contain all of Poe's tales, his poems, and his excellent literary criticism as well as a highly moving selection of his letters. For added entertainment it also includes Griswold's damning memoir, which should be regarded as a work of comedy. The essay by Poe's friend N. P. Willis also includes the whole of Griswold's announcement of Poe's death in the *New York Tribune*, another piece of humorous fiction.

N. Bryllion Fagin, *The Histrionic Mr. Poe* (Johns Hopkins University Press, 1967). This work takes the opposite approach to Quinn's comprehensive biography, attempting to examine the theatrical quality of so much of Poe's behavior, and how this affected his work. Fagin claims that "many of [Poe's] poems, stories and essays are quite clearly theatrical performances," and he analyzes them and their author accordingly. Among other things, he takes into account such elements as Poe's appearance and his voice when he gave public readings, and how these may have affected his writing. Here is a compelling account of how Poe often lost himself in his own creations.

Edgar Allan Poe, *Eureka* (Prometheus Books, 1997). Poe's controversial "essay on the spiritual and material universe," which in this edition contains an intriguing and perceptive foreword by the celebrated British astronomer Sir Patrick Moore. Poe's hundred or so pages contain the summation of his scientific and metaphysical theories concerning the "unity" of the universe. Nonsense or brilliance, or a perplexing mixture of both—a couple of hours' reading will enable you to decide for yourself.

Arthur Hobson Quinn, *Edgar Allan Poe: A Critical Biography* (Johns Hopkins University Press, 1997). The best readily available comprehensive biography. Quinn's meticulous research in the family archives and other pertinent locations unearthed all manner of arcane facts about Poe's life, separating the man from his much-embellished legend. He also offers a good, level-headed analysis of almost all of Poe's tales and poems. Eight hundred pages of Poe's life and work, and nothing but.

Philip Van Doren Stern, ed., *The Viking Portable Poe* (Penguin, 1977). By far the best and most comprehensive selection of Poe's works. Poems include all his best-known verses, from masterpieces such as "Ulalume" and "The Raven" to the enigmatic "To My Mother." Also includes many of his classic tales as well as a selection of letters and criticism. Its only defect is the omission of a selection from *Eureka*, which was disregarded at the time.

Index

A NOTE ON THE AUTHOR

Paul Strathern has lectured in philosophy and mathematics and now lives and writes in London. He is the author of the enormously successful series Philosophers in 90 Minutes. A Somerset Maugham Prize winner, he is also the author of books on history and travel, as well as five novels. His articles have appeared in a great many publications, including the *Observer* (London) and the *Irish Times*.

Paul Strathern's 90 Minutes series in philosophy, also published by Ivan R. Dee, includes individual books on Thomas Aquinas, Aristotle, St. Augustine, Berkeley, Confucius, Derrida, Descartes, Dewey, Foucault, Hegel, Heidegger, Hume, Kant, Kierkegaard, Leibniz, Locke, Machiavelli, Marx, J. S. Mill, Nietzsche, Plato, Rousseau, Bertrand Russell, Sartre, Schopenhauer, Socrates, Spinoza, and Wittgenstein.

NOW PUBLISHED IN THIS SERIES:

Beckett in 90 Minutes
Borges in 90 Minutes
Dostoevsky in 90 Minutes
Hemingway in 90 Minutes
James Joyce in 90 Minutes
Kafka in 90 Minutes
D. H. Lawrence in 90 Minutes
García Márquez in 90 Minutes
Nabokov in 90 Minutes
Poe in 90 Minutes
Tolstoy in 90 Minutes
Virginia Woolf in 90 Minutes

IN PREPARATION:

Jane Austen, Balzac, Bellow, Brecht, Camus, Cather, Cervantes, Chekhov, Conrad, Dante, Dickens, Faulkner, Fitzgerald, Flaubert, Gogol, Grass, Hardy, Hugo, Huxley, Ibsen, Henry James, Kipling, Mailer, Mann, Melville, Montaigne, Orwell, Proust, Shakespeare, Silone, Singer, Solzhenitsyn, Stendhal, Stevenson, Turgenev, Twain, Vonnegut, Whitman, Zola